FACTOR WORDS

A Collection of The O'Reilly Factor's
Favorite "Words of the Day"

BY

BILL O'REILLY
AND THE O'REILLY FACTOR STAFF

Factor Words: A Collection of The O'Reilly Factor's Favorite "Words of the Day"

Cover design and page layouts by Ryan Eanes
Example sentences by Paul Budline and Kristin Lazure
Research by Trish Monte
Copy editing by Todd Wachsman

Cover photo by Carolyn Cole. Copyright © 2010 Los Angeles Times. Reprinted with permission.
Back cover photo by Anthony Brown/iStockphoto.com
Bill O'Reilly headshot by Lynn McCann Youngen, courtesy of Bill O'Reilly
Book stack photo by Lichtmeister/Bigstock.com

ISBN-13 978-1-4507-8978-3 case-bound hardcover

Distributed directly to the public by BillOReilly.com

This book is dedicated to loyal Factor viewers, Premium Members,
and those who so generously support The Factor's ongoing charitable work.

Special thanks to David Tabacoff, John Barnsworthy and Jeff Schiffman.

INTRODUCTION

It all began with a teed off Factor viewer who emailed me demanding to know why I used the word 'perspicacious,' and asking what it meant. I read the criticism with an open mind, remembering one of my journalism professors telling me never to use big words on TV because if the audience doesn't know the word's meaning, they'll be angry with you.

But, instead of following the professor's advice, I decided to expand my use of big and obscure words because they're fun. Presto—the Factor's "word of the day" came into being.

Our research shows the most commonly used words of the day are bloviate, pecksniffian, mendacious, popinjay, blooter, poltroon, blatherskite, jackanapes, and ninnyhammer. All are defined in this volume.

The one thing those words have in common is that they are all negative. And I get mail on that as well. "Can't you have some positive words of the day, O'Reilly?" Well, don't be truculent! Negative words are simply more entertaining than positive words. Or maybe I'm just a curmudgeon.

I hope you enjoy this adventure in vocabulary and pass the words along to your kids, grandkids, or some urchin who is annoying you on a plane. The English language is slowly truncating, and we must fight that insidious trend. We must be warriors in the army of the lexicon.

Finally, thanks for buying this book. Your perspicacity is now assured.

FACTOR WORDS

**A Collection of The O'Reilly Factor's
Favorite "Words of the Day"**

agog

uh-GOG

adj. curious; eager

Almost everyone was **agog** when the uninvited couple strolled into the state dinner at the White House.

autocratic

aw-tuh-KRAT-ick

adj. acting like someone who has undisputed power or authority

When he expressed an opinion they deemed offensive, his **autocratic** bosses at NPR swung the proverbial axe.

balderdash

BALL-dur-dash

n. nonsense; stupidity

Oh, **balderdash**! How can the Speaker of the House claim her excessive use of a taxpayer-funded private jet was to the benefit of the American people?

barbermonger

BAR-bur-mung-ur

n. a vain or superficial man

A certain haughty, wind-surfing presidential candidate picked a **barbermonger** as his running mate.

bellicose

BELL-uh-kose

adj. aggressive; combative

A handful of **bellicose** protesters disrupted the Congressional hearings with their loud shouts and taunts.

bilge

BILJ

n. stupid talk or writing; silliness

Most arguments against Jessica's Law
consisted of unadulterated **bilge**.

bilious

BIL-yus

adj. ill-tempered; unpleasant

The senator's **bilious** and over-the-top rant against his opponent led voters to reconsider whether he had the composure and class necessary to be commander-in-chief.

blatherskite

BLATH-ur-skite

n. a foolish and overly talkative person

Why did the **blatherskite** cross the road?
To drone on and bore more folks on the other side.

blooter

BLOO-tur

n. a fool; an **oaf**; a blunderer

When writing to The Factor, you may come off as a complete **blooter** if you forget to include your name and town with your correspondence.

bloviate

BLOW-vee-ate

v. to speak at length; to prattle on

It's better to remain silent and be thought a fool than to **bloviate** and remove all doubt. (With apologies to Honest Abe.)

boorish

BOOR-ish

adj. uncultured; crude

Your humble correspondent has been accused of **boorish** behavior, but The Factor's format mandates that guests who attempt to deceive the viewer with spin must be interrupted.

bovine

BOH-vine

adj. obtuse; dull; slow

CNN, once the dominant player in cable news, now seems positively **bovine** compared to FNC's vibrancy.

braggadocio

brag-uh-DOH-show

n. hollow self-praise; boasting

It was nothing but **braggadocio** when Libyan dictator Moammar Qaddafi insisted his corrupt regime could not possibly be brought down by international forces.

brazen

BRAY-zen

adj. shameless; without modesty

She was **brazen** enough to believe she could waltz into the No Spin Zone and get away with dodging questions.

buffoon

buh-FOON

n. a fool; a trickster

Late-night comedians often acted like a bunch of **buffoons** throughout the entire Bush administration, constantly belittling the president and all things conservative.

bumpkin

BUMP-kin

n. a hick; a yokel

Secular progressives tend to view religious folks
as poor, dumb **bumpkins**.

bumptious

BUMP-shus

adj. overly assertive; offensively conceited

Level-headed folks aren't swayed by the ridiculous arguments that **bumptious** 9/11 conspiracy theorists continue to spout.

bunkum

BUNG-kum

n. empty rhetoric; blarney

The word "**bunkum**" is actually derived from the name of Buncombe County in North Carolina, where a certain politician was infamous for speaking pure twaddle.

cacophonous

kuh-KOFF-uh-nuss

adj. harsh and unpleasant-sounding

The **cacophonous** chorus of Code Pink protesters drowned out rational discussion when they stood up and shouted down the general's Congressional testimony on the war in Afghanistan.

callow

KAL-oh

adj. immature; green; naïve

In America, even the most **callow** small-town boy can grow up to be a famous and humble correspondent.

cantankerous

can-TANK-ur-us

adj. ill-tempered and quarrelsome; disagreeable

The defendant's father took the stand for the prosecution, but his **cantankerous** demeanor led the jury to look at him and his testimony with suspicion.

capricious

kuh-PREE-shus

adj. led by fancy or impulse

Courts have ruled that the death penalty,
if applied in a **capricious** and unpredictable manner,
violates the Constitution.

caterwauling

KAT-ur-wall-ing

n. a cry or screech like a female cat in heat

Many folks remember unscrupulous televangelists **caterwauling** and crying during their broadcasts as they begged for donations.

caustic

KAW-stick

adj. biting; sarcastic; dry

His many **caustic** reviews earned Frank Rich the infamous title of "Butcher of Broadway."

charlatan

SHAR-luh-tin

n. a fraud; a quack

When it comes to politics, there are far too many **charlatans** out there trying to line their own pockets while they pretend to look out for the folks.

choleric

kuh-LEHR-ick

adj. irritable; easily angered; hot-tempered

General Patton, known for his **choleric** outbursts, was reprimanded when he slapped a soldier in 1943.

chuffiness

CHUFF-ee-ness

adj. churlishness; boorishness

The gubernatorial candidate approached the situation regarding his alleged illegal alien employees with a **chuffiness** that was beneath the office he sought.

churlish

CHURL-ish

adj. rude; surly; vulgar

In addition to being incompetent, the tech support guy had the gall to get **churlish** when asked a question.

clinchpoop

KLINCH-poop

n. a moronic person

A word of warning: don't be a **clinchpoop** and write letters of complaint to The Factor without backing up your beef with solid facts and examples.

codger

KODJ-ur

n. an odd older man

To qualify as a **codger**, it helps to be elderly and a bit odd, and it's absolutely mandatory to have a Y chromosome.

codswallop

CODZ-wol-up

n. flim-flam; nonsense; garbage

After a careful review of the defense team's arguments, The Factor's legal analysts have concluded the defendant is guilty and her insanity plea is **codswallop**.

conniption

cun-NIP-shun

n. hysterics; a state of extreme agitation

The woman seemed quite unstable, having a laughing **conniption** one minute and flying into a **conniption** of rage the next.

contentious

cun-TEN-shus

adj. argumentative; quarrelsome

What started as a mere disagreement about a controversy within the Miss USA pageant eventually erupted into a **contentious** war of words between real estate mogul Donald Trump and talk show veteran Rosie O'Donnell.

contumacious

kon-too-MAY-shus

adj. willfully disobedient; insubordinate

With its insistence on conformity and deference to authority, the Army is not the best place for a **contumacious** young man.

coxcomb

COX-comb

n. a person who is showy and superficial

Former presidential candidate John Edwards revealed himself to be a true **coxcomb** in the Internet video where he's caught combing his hair to perfection for several minutes.

craven

CRAY-ven

adj. totally without courage; fearful

He was invited on the show to defend his position, but the **craven** politician elected to hide under his desk.

cretin

KREE-tin

n. a person who behaves in a stupid or moronic manner

The BP CEO's weekend sailing trip during the oil spill crisis sparked anger and made him look like an apathetic **cretin**.

curmudgeon

ker-MUHJ-un

n. a cranky, disagreeable and stubborn person

The peevish economist was known to be a disagreeable **curmudgeon** long before he was awarded the Nobel Prize.

derisive

dih-RIH-siv

adj. contemptuous; disdainful

The plaintiff who sought to have the words "under God" legally removed from the Pledge of Allegiance had such a **derisive** tone that his cause failed to garner many supporters.

diabolical

dy-uh-BOL-ik-ul

adj. extraordinarily fiendish or evil

Only the most **diabolical** villain could devise a plot using commercial jetliners to kill thousands of innocents.

discombobulated

dis-kum-BOB-yoo-lay-tid

v. to upset or confuse

When Lady Gaga appeared onstage at an awards show wearing a dress made entirely of steak, the spectacle certainly **discombobulated** the audience.

disputatious

dis-pyoo-TAY-shus

adj. argumentative; combative

Unless you are fond of frequent arguments, marry a **disputatious** spouse at your peril.

dogmatic

dawg-MAT-ick

adj. given to forcibly spouting opinions as if they were facts

The *New York Times'* **dogmatic** pro-amnesty, open-border stance has turned off many readers who oppose illegal immigration and has led to an avalanche of cancelled subscriptions.

doltish

DOHLT-ish

adj. stupid; idiotic

I felt kind of **doltish** after getting every question wrong on the Great American News Quiz.

doofus

DOO-fuss

n. an idiot; a fool

Only a **doofus** would squander all of his time on pointless diversions instead of working hard for a better life.

dumbledore

DUM-bul-dore

n. a busybody

J.K. Rowling named the headmaster in the *Harry Potter* books "Albus Dumbledore," perhaps considering him an actual **dumbledore** who got involved in everything.

dunderhead

DUN-durr-head

n. a dolt; an incredibly stupid person

Christian conservative groups consider the California state government to be a bunch of **dunderheads** for mandating that students be taught about gay history in the classroom.

enigma

uh-NIG-muh

n. a mystery; a perplexing situation

Asked about Russia, Churchill described the communist nation as "a riddle wrapped in a mystery inside an **enigma**."

fallacious

fuh-LAY-shus

adj. deceptive; deceitful

When Democrats make their case for tax hikes for the wealthy, they use **fallacious** economic arguments to hide their true intention of income redistribution.

fatuous

FATCH-oo-us

adj. silly; vapid; inane

The president's zealous admirers treat even his most **fatuous** comments as if they were delivered by Zeus on a thunderbolt.

feckless

FECK-less

adj. incompetent; lazy; lacking in purpose

The Culture Warriors have tried, time and again,
to explain what's behind the new trend among **feckless** teens
who text photos of themselves drinking and misbehaving.

fey

FAY

adj. whimsical; odd; unreal

People described as **fey** usually seem to be living in a different world—a world with just one slightly off-kilter inhabitant.

flapdoodle

FLAP-doo-dul

n. foolish talk; nonsense

One of The Factor's most popular segments is "Miller Time" because of Dennis' unique style that combines both insight and funny **flapdoodle**.

flummery

FLUM-uh-ree

n. a lack of any meaning; nonsense

The debate over tax cuts overflowed with **flummery** and outright deceit on both sides.

flummoxed

FLUM-muxed

adj. confused; perplexed

Officials at the Berlin Zoo were **flummoxed** by the sudden death of their star polar bear Knut, who was relatively young when he collapsed.

foofaraw

FOO-fur-raw

n. an uproar or fuss over something unimportant or inconsequential

Academic debates are marked by much **foofaraw** precisely because there is so little at stake.

fop

FOP

n. one who is excessively refined and vain

As you know, your humble correspondent isn't very interested in hob-nobbing with Hollywood **fops**, but is much more comfortable hanging with the regular folks.

fractious

FRAK-shus

adj. stubborn; difficult

As the Yankee crowd grew louder and more **fractious**, the Boston fan wisely removed his Red Sox cap.

fuddy-duddy

FUD-ee-dud-ee

n. a picky, uptight or stuffy person

Despite his popular platform, the former governor's campaign for the presidency failed to catch fire because voters perceived him as a **fuddy-duddy** lacking charisma.

furciferous

fur-SIFF-ur-us

adj. scandalous; dishonorable; contemptible

Like Charles Ponzi before him, the **furciferous** Bernie Madoff created a cunning pyramid scheme.

furtive

FUR-tiv

adj. stealthy; clandestine; shifty

During the debate, cameras caught the senator shooting a **furtive** glance at her advisor whenever her opponent botched an answer.

garrulous

GARE-yuh-luhs

adj. wordy; excessively verbose

After a couple of drinks, he turned from verecund to talkative; a few more glasses, and he was downright **garrulous**.

gasconading

gas-cuh-NEYD-ing

v. to excessively brag

After the soirée with the royal couple, there was plenty of **gasconading** amongst the party-goers about who got the most face time with the glamorous prince and duchess.

gnarly

NAR-lee

adj. gross; nasty

The old guy with **gnarly** hands had a personality to match.

gongoozler

gon-GOOZ-lur

n. a passive observer

Whether you agree or disagree with the tactics of the Minutemen, who have established armed watches at the Mexican border, you have to admire the fact that they're not **gongoozlers** when it comes to protecting this country from the threat of rampant illegal immigrantion.

gormless

GORM-less

adj. lacking intelligence

The reality show "The Simple Life" turned **gormless** socialites into TV stars.

hackneyed

HACK-need

adj. overused; common; stale

The **hackneyed** arguments to try the 9/11 ringleader in New York City civilian court didn't hold water, so the Obama administration changed its mind and opted for a military tribunal instead.

honeyfuggle

HUN-ee-fug-gull

v. to dupe or deceive by flattery;
to obtain by deception

Sorry to bring him up again, but no one could **honeyfuggle**
a potential investor like Bernie Madoff could.

hooligan

HOO-li-guhn

n. a thug; a ruffian

The World Trade Organization conference in 1999 is best remembered for the band of angry **hooligans** who violently demonstrated in the streets of Seattle, causing millions of dollars' worth of damage.

hornswoggle

HORN-swog-gle

v. to cheat; to hoax; to defraud

Selling the Brooklyn Bridge was once considered the ultimate **hornswoggle**; now it may be a politician pledging to cut the budget deficit.

hubris

HYOO-bris

n. an excessively inflated sense of pride, self-confidence or ego

Even though our analysis of the speculators' manipulation of oil prices has been spot on, Talking Points will refrain from displaying **hubris** if prices at the pump spike to reflect our theory.

imperious

im-PEER-ee-us

adj. haughty; tyrannical; dictatorial

"I am in control here," declared the **imperious** Secretary of State.

impudent

IM-pyoo-dent

adj. disrespectful; insolent; contemptuous

Even some of Sarah Palin's staunchest critics found it **impudent** for the author who was writing a book about the former governor to buy the property next door to her family home in Alaska.

indolent

IN-doh-lent

adj. lazy; slothful

An entitlement state, with money taken from some folks and given to others, can lead people to be **indolent** and dependent.

insipid

in-SIP-id

adj. dull; lacking any apparent or interesting qualities

Actor Sean Penn is so **insipid** that he clamors for public attention by engaging in outlandish publicity stunts like meeting with the anti-American Venezuelan dictator Hugo Chavez.

insolent

IN-suh-lent

adj. disrespectful; rude

Back when Bill was a high school teacher, a defiant student might be **insolent** once, but never twice!

invidious

in-VID-ee-us

adj. intended to create animosity or resentment

The former candidate stormed off the set during a televised interview because she found the line of questioning to be **invidious** and insulting.

irascible

ih-RAS-uh-bul

adj. testy; irritable

The imperious CEO grew **irascible** as the Congressional panel peppered him with what he felt were insolent questions.

jabberwocky

JAB-ur-wok-ee

n. nonsensical speech or writing; gibberish

When anti-American dictators are given a platform to speak to the world at the United Nations headquarters, it often turns into long-winded **jabberwocky** about the "evils" of the United States.

jackanapes

JACK-uh-napes

n. a silly person with a ridiculous air

The Factor endeavors to explore all sides of the issues, because only a **jackanapes** would refuse to consider opinions aside from his or her own.

japery

JAYP-ur-ee

n. a joke; a mockery

The Harry Potter fanatics who dress in wizard gear and camp out for days to buy the latest book or see the latest movie are just a **japery**—don't they have anything better to do?

jejune

juh-JOON

adj. uninteresting; dull

The book was merely tedious, but the movie adaptation was positively **jejune**.

jobbernowl

JOB-bur-nowl

n. a stupid person

Your humble correspondent assumed the rock star would be a **jobbernowl** who couldn't defend his outspoken radical political views, so I was pleasantly surprised when he appeared on the Factor and had an intelligent debate with me.

lemming

LEMM-ing

n. someone who follows the crowd without thinking

The ultimate **lemmings** were Jim Jones' followers, who followed him blindly and literally drank the poison-spiked Kool-Aid.

lethargic

luh-THAR-jik

adj. sleepy; sluggish; drowsy

Murder charges against the single mother are forthcoming after she failed to seek medical attention for her sick and **lethargic** infant, resulting in the baby's tragic death.

lilliputian

lil-i-PYOO-shun

adj. insignificant; petty

Ronald Reagan had a way of making his opponents seem **lilliputian** by comparison.

lily-livered

LILL-ee LIV-ered

adj. cowardly; timid

The **lily-livered** Internet blogger who repeatedly attacked The Factor refused to come on the show to explain her beef... so we sent producer Jesse Watters to her!

lollygagging

LOL-ee-gagg-ing

v. to spend time idly

I intended to create sentences for this book, but instead spent the day **lollygagging**. Maybe tomorrow!

loquacious

loh-KWAY-shus

adj. talkative; wordy

If you get too **loquacious** in answering questions in the
No Spin Zone, I will ask you to get to the point, as this is a
fast-paced program—we don't have time to dawdle.

lugubrious

loo-GOO-bree-us

adj. sorrowful; gloomy

When the ratings came out, the hallways of the low-rated cable network were filled with **lugubrious** expressions and a funereal atmosphere.

luminary

LOO-muh-ner-ee

n. a person who is inspirational to others

While many consider Al Gore a **luminary** for his work on behalf of the environment, there have been legitimate questions raised about whether the high profits he's earned from his crusade make it a purely altruistic endeavor.

malevolent

muh–LEV–uh–lent

adj. malicious; evil

The James Bond movies featured a series of extraordinary villains, each one more **malevolent** than the last.

martinet

mar-tin-ET

n. a person who strictly adheres to the rules

The moderator of the presidential debate flustered the candidates by being a strict **martinet** when it came to time limits, often cutting the participants off mid-sentence.

maudlin

MAWD-lin

adj. shallowly emotional or sentimental

Some drunks get boisterous and cheery,
while others grow **maudlin** and teary.

mawkish

MAWK-ish

adj. excessively and insincerely sentimental; falsely emotional

In front of the judge, the troubled young actress pretended to be contrite (but came off as completely **mawkish**) in order to win sympathy and a lenient sentence.

mendacious

men-DAY-shus

adj. false; dishonest

The defense team conceded that Casey Anthony was **mendacious** about everything, but insisted that lying doesn't make you a killer.

meretricious

mer-uh-TRISH-us

adj. trashy; vulgar

The beauty queen made the rounds on the talk show circuit, always wearing bright, **meretricious** attire to attract as much continued media attention as possible.

misanthrope

MIS-uhn-thrope

n. a person with an aversion to other people and society

With their hatred of modernity and their criticism of humans, some environmentalists seem to be full-fledged **misanthropes**.

miscreant

MIS-kree-unt

n. an evildoer; a person without morals

After the mysterious disappearance of American teen Natalee Holloway in Aruba, a Dutch **miscreant** named Joran van der Sloot gained notoriety for his involvement in the case.

mooncalf

MOON-caff

n. a person who foolishly daydreams

For a mendacious investment adviser, there is only one thing better than a **mooncalf**—a rich **mooncalf**.

mordant

MORE-dint

adj. sarcastic; caustic; sharp

After Charlie Sheen's **mordant** diatribe against his
"Two and a Half Men" producer, the troubled actor was fired
from the sitcom and his popular character killed off
in a bizarre freak accident.

morose

muh-ROHS

adj. gloomy; sulky

After being booted from office in a testy recall election, the disgraced governor grew **morose** and sullen.

mugwump

MUG-wump

n. a person who remains undecided or noncommittal

As the Democratic candidate's position on gay marriage evolved to align with public opinion, there were growing accusations that his flip-flopping on social issues made him a **mugwump**.

namby-pamby

NAM-bee PAM-bee

n. a weak, insipid, cowardly person

Michele Bachmann, declaring that she is no **namby-pamby**, boasted to Bill about her "titanium spine."

nebbish

NEBB-ish

n. a weak or timid person; a simpleton

Former classmates of the accused gunman recall the suspect as being a loner and a **nebbish**, a guy who rarely talked to anyone else and never had any friends.

nebulous

NEB-you-lus

adj. unclear; vague

The presidential candidate hypnotized crowds with his soaring rhetoric, even though his proposals were **nebulous** at best.

nefarious

ni-FAIR-ee-us

adj. very evil or heinous

Only **nefarious** individuals with no moral compass would attempt to scam victims of natural disasters like tornadoes or earthquakes for their own personal gain.

neolithic

NEE-uh-lith-ik

adj. ancient; outmoded

Elites in the mainstream media like to portray traditional Americans as backward and **neolithic**.

nimiety

ni-MAY-i-tee

n. an excess; too much of something

The debate about the estate tax was marked by a **nimiety** of socialistic rhetoric by the liberal commentator about the rich having to spread their wealth around to the less fortunate.

nimrod

NIM-rod

n. a person regarded as silly, foolish, or stupid

After decades of grade inflation, you'd have to be a **nimrod** or a lollygagger to flunk out of an Ivy League university.

ninnyhammer

NINN-ee-hamm-ur

n. a foolish person

A career criminal who robs the home of a police sergeant immediately after being released from prison is a **ninnyhammer** who deserves a few more years behind bars... and that's exactly what he'll get!

nit-pick

NIT-pik

v. to find fault with minor or unimportant details

If your fiancée ignores all of your inarguably superior features and constantly **nit-picks** at one teeny-tiny flaw, think twice about taking the plunge.

nitwit

NIT-wit

n. a dolt; a stupid person

Only a **nitwit** would set out to climb Mount Rainier in the middle of a blizzard—the end result will simply be hundreds of thousands of taxpayer dollars spent on a futile rescue mission.

noddy

NOD-ee

n. a dunce; a silly person

Q: What's the difference between a nimrod,
a blatherskite, a mooncalf, and a **noddy**?
A: Not much; none of them can understand the question.

nugatory

NOO-guh-tor-ee

adj. worthless; invalid

Because the liberal polling outfit tends to survey
Americans who share its left-leaning opinions,
its latest poll showing the Democratic incumbent
as a heavy favorite is largely **nugatory**.

objurgate

OB-jer-gait

v. to pointedly or angrily scold

The irascible actor lost his cool and proceeded to **objurgate** his 13-year-old daughter.

oblique

ub-LEEK

adj. indirect; unclear

Economists were forecasting no improvement in the unemployment figures, while the administration was putting out **oblique** statistics showing job creation to calm the nation's fears.

obsequious

ub-SEE-kwee-us

adj. excessively deferential

A competent CEO surrounds himself with independent thinkers, not **obsequious** lemmings.

obtuse

ub-TOOSE

adj. slow to understand; unperceptive

The heat blanketing the Northeast must be making some people **obtuse** because there was a real lack of energy at the recent town hall meetings about the economic downturn.

odious

OH-dee-us

adj. repulsive; disgusting

The anti-war rally featured **odious** signs depicting
the president as a latter-day Hitler.

palter

PAWL-ter

v. to equivocate; to act dishonestly

Martha Stewart's unwise decision to **palter** over her stock purchase resulted in a very public stint in a minimum-security prison.

parsimonious

par-suh-MOH-nee-us

adj. frugal; cheap; miserly

His players accused the **parsimonious** team owner of tossing around nickels like they were manhole covers.

pawky

PAW-kee

adj. shrewd; cunning

It was a **pawky** move for some in the Tea Party crowd to start circulating the idea of impeachment for the president if he didn't get the debt deal done in a timely fashion.

peccant

PEK-unt

adj. guilty of sin

The Bible warns the **peccant** among us to repent or face eternal damnation.

pecksniffian

peck-SNIFF-ee-un

adj. sanctimonious; falsely moralistic

The liberal pundit took a **pecksniffian** tone when arguing in favor of an amnesty plan, but the truth is that nobody is calling for mass deportations of otherwise law-abiding illegal immigrants.

pedantic

puh-DAN-tick

adj. displaying an obsession with tiny details

The more narrow and **pedantic** the teacher, the less inspired and creative the student.

pedestrian

puh-DES-tree-un

adj. unoriginal; uninspiring

The formula for many news programs has become so predictable and **pedestrian** that it's no wonder more and more Americans are turning to Fox News for something fresh and exciting.

peevish

PEE-vish

adj. discontent; irritable

The **peevish** hosts actually stormed off the set when a guest accurately pointed out that Muslims flew planes into the World Trade Center.

pejorative

pi-JOR-uh-tiv

adj. contemptuous

As the bitter breakup of one of Hollywood's longest lasting couples descended into **pejorative** insults and accusations, the tabloid media worked itself up into a frenzy covering the sensational story.

perfidious

per-FID-ee-us

adj. traitorous; treacherous

He seemed pious and honest, but the preacher turned out to be as **perfidious** as Satan himself.

pernicious

per-NISH-us

adj. hurtful; destructive

British superstar Simon Cowell made a career out of **pernicious** critiques of aspiring young singers on the hit show "American Idol."

persnickety

per-SNICK-i-tee

adj. finicky; fussy

Many rock stars are notorious for their **persnickety** demands about precisely what must be in their dressing room.

perspicacious

pur-spi-KAY-shus

adj. sharp; perceptive

In my first sit-down with the former presidential candidate, I found her to have an exceedingly **perspicacious** mind when it came to analyzing complex issues.

pestiferous

pes-TIFF-ur-us

adj. annoying; bothersome; irritating

Tsetse flies can be deadly,
but houseflies are merely **pestiferous**.

pettifogger

PET-ee-fah-gur

n. someone who uses petty and unscrupulous tactics

While some have labeled the disgruntled flight attendant a **pettifogger** for escaping his plane via the emergency slide, others fully understood his frustration and supported his antics.

petulant

PET-yoo-lunt

adj. irritable; insolent

The **petulant** child screamed and wailed inconsolably when he was told that he couldn't have any ice cream for dessert.

philistine

FIL-uh-steen

adj. lacking culture; dismissive of society

Philistine attitudes abound amongst American teenagers who seem to favor wasting time with video games and electronics over more worthwhile endeavors like reading.

picayune

pick-uh-YOON

adj. insignificant; trivial

The Picayune was a Spanish coin with very little value; not surprisingly, the word "**picayune**" is synonymous with insignificance and triviality.

pinhead

PIN-head

n. a person who is stupid or doltish

If you hurt children, betray the United States, or defame innocent people, you will automatically be branded a **pinhead** for life in the No Spin Zone.

pithy

PITH-ee

adj. brief; concise

As everyone knows, letters are far more likely to be read if they are **pithy** and pointed, not wordy and nebulous.

poltroon

pole-TROON

n. a spineless coward

The Internet seems to be full of **poltroons** who delight in hurling insults and invective—but only when they can remain anonymous behind their keyboards.

popinjay

POP-in-jay

n. a vain and overly talkative person; a chatterbox

I got stuck next to a **popinjay** who spent the entire flight combing his hair and talking about jejune subjects.

porcine

pour-SEEN

adj. reminiscent of a pig or hog

The gluttonous and **porcine** Mr. Creosote from the Monty Python movie "The Meaning of Life" met a messy demise when he couldn't keep himself from overindulging.

priggish

PRIG-gish

adj. overly detail-oriented; particular

The mighty British Empire was, in effect, run by overly proper and **priggish** civil servants who slavishly enforced every rule.

procacity

pro-CASS-ih-tee

n. arrogance; impudence; petulance

In the business of entertainment reporting, a temperament marked by **procacity** and assertiveness is beneficial when trying to nab red carpet interviews with in-demand celebrities.

procrustean

pro-KRUS-tee-un

adj. violent enforcement of uniformity

Labor bosses despise the secret ballot; they prefer a **procrustean** "card check" system that pressures workers to endorse a union.

prudish

PROO-dish

adj. overly modest; prim

The "Church Lady," Dana Carvey's character from "Saturday Night Live," is a pitch-perfect parody of **prudish** tastes taken to the extreme.

puerile

PYOOR-ile

adj. childish; immature; infantile

Most of the Bush-bashing bumper stickers were **puerile**,
totally lacking in sophistication or humor.

pugnacious

pug-NAY-shus

adj. combative; argumentative

Though the two men are said to be fond of each other personally, the exchanges between John McCain and Barack Obama during their run for the White House had a tendency to get a bit hostile and **pugnacious**.

puzzlewit

PUHZ-ul-wit

n. a stupid, dimwitted person

Ironically, a **puzzlewit** can't solve a simple puzzle…
and has absolutely no wit.

quakebuttock

KWAYK-butt-uck

n. a sniveling coward

The Somali pirate sure acted brave while he was armed with an AK-47, but he turned into a **quakebuttock** as soon as he entered the courtroom to face charges.

querulous

KWER-yoo-lus

adj. whiny; constantly complaining

The day after the wedding she went from agreeable to **querulous**, complaining about everything from his clothing to his snoring.

quidnunc

KWID-nunk

n. a blabbermouth; a gossip

The Congressman has proven himself to be a real **quidnunc**, more interested in trafficking in Beltway gossip than in working to solve his constituents' problems.

quixotic

kwik-SOT-ic

adj. impulsive; unrealistic

At first blush, it seemed **quixotic** that a first-term senator with no executive experience would run for the White House.

rambunctious

ram-BUNK-shus

adj. boisterous; wild; out of control

Rambunctious hockey fans in Canada reacted to their team's tough loss by rioting in the streets, prompting police to use rubber bullets and tear gas to get the crowd under control.

rapscallion

rap-SKAL-yun

n. a rogue; a charlatan

Much of his wayward youth was spent in a pool hall, hanging around with drunks, thieves and assorted **rapscallions**.

recalcitrant

ree-KALSE-uh-trant

adj. stubborn; defiant

The lingering debt deadlock was marked by **recalcitrant** politicians on both sides of the aisle who refused to compromise in the best interests of the country.

restive

RESS-tiv

adj. edgy; tense; jittery

The crowd was **restive** to begin with, but the firebrand's speech pushed them over the edge.

sagacious

suh-GAY-shus

adj. insightful; discerning

Strict constructionists believe the Founding Fathers were **sagacious** men whose writings were timeless and whose values still apply today.

sapid

SAP-id

adj. agreeable; appealing

Great food is **sapid** to the taste buds, great literature **sapid** to the mind, and great Factor gear **sapid** to the eyes.

saturnine

SAT-ur-nine

adj. bitter; gloomy; surly

The mood in the politician's office was **saturnine** following his televised admission that he had in fact engaged in inappropriate behavior on the Internet.

scelestious

skuh-LESS-tee-us

adj. wicked or evil

The challenge for young Mr. Potter was discerning which wizards were righteous and which were **scelestious**.

scurrilous

SKURR-uh-lus

adj. outrageously insulting;
obscenely defamatory

The newspaper's ombudsman had some choice words to
say about the opinion columnist whose previous article had
contained shockingly **scurrilous** invective aimed at
a minority group.

skullduggery

skul-DUG-uh-ree

n. deception; trickery; deceit

With President Nixon cruising toward an easy re-election, there was no need for his "plumbers" to resort to **skullduggery**.

snarky

SNAR-kee

adj. crabby; sarcastic

After leaving the White House, Bill Clinton has sometimes gotten very **snarky** when asked about the Monica Lewinsky scandal that led to his historic impeachment.

snippy

SNIP-ee

adj. blunt; curt

When the candidates started bickering on the phone about the Florida results, Gore demanded that Bush stop being so **snippy**.

snollygoster

SNOLL-ee-gos-tur

n. a person who is unprincipled or shrewd

The **snollygosters** in the New Black Panthers who stood outside a polling place in 2008 waving billy clubs were never prosecuted for voter intimidation, but they should have been.

somnambulant

som-NAM-byoo-lent

n., adj. a sleepwalker; one who sleepwalks

Medical experts were baffled when they learned that many users of prescription sleep aids engage in **somnambulant** feasts, sometimes even gorging on inedible or dangerous substances.

sop

SOP

n. a person who is cowardly or timid

Michael Jackson supporters deny the pop star would ever have harmed a child and say the molestation charges against him were leveled by a **sop** looking to cash in on her son's friendship with the international star.

sophist

SOF-ist

n. a person who uses elaborate and deceptive arguments

It took a truly skilled **sophist** to convince the jury that the comely mom did not kill her infant daughter.

spurious

SPYOOR-ee-us

adj. counterfeit; illegitimate

After Bin Laden was discovered near a military complex in Pakistan, many Americans wondered if the alliance between our country and theirs was **spurious**.

superbious

soo-PURB-ee-us

adj. proud; arrogant; overbearing

Some fans felt LeBron James was acting **superbious** when he staged a TV spectacular to announce his decision to play for Miami.

supercilious

soo-per-SILL-ee-us

adj. showing arrogance or contempt

President Nixon's initial refusal to release the Watergate tapes to a Senate committee, claiming they were vital to national security, was a **supercilious** move for which he was harshly judged by the American public.

surly

SUR-lee

adj. mean; ill-tempered

TSA agents are almost uniformly cordial, but we've all run into a few **surly** ones as well.

sycophant

SICK-oh-fant

n. a yes-man; a fawning minion

Powerful people like Oprah Winfrey have to be extra cautious not to surround themselves with **sycophants** who don't really have their best interests at heart.

tedious

TEE-dee-us

adj. endlessly boring

I left my copy of *Pinheads and Patriots* at home, making the flight all the more **tedious**.

temerity

tuh-MER-i-tee

n. gall; audacity

Refusing to heed tsunami warnings by not seeking shelter on higher ground is a sign of **temerity** that can have deadly consequences.

temulent

TIM-yoo-lent

adj. drunk or intoxicated

Lots of folks suspect Charlie Sheen was **temulent** when he sat down for a series of bizarre television interviews.

tendentious

ten-DEN-shus

adj. biased; partisan

The Factor tries to avoid giving a platform to strictly **tendentious** individuals who stick to their partisan talking points and refuse to listen to reason.

tenuous

TEN-yoo-uhs

adj. questionable; vague

Keynesians say more government spending leads to more employment, but the link is **tenuous** at best.

terse

TURSE

adj. succinct; pithy

George Washington's **terse** inaugural address in 1793 was the shortest in presidential history, in which he simply expressed his commitment to the oath of office.

thewless

THEW-less

adj. lacking in energy; weak

Answer: The shoeless, clueless, and **thewless**.
Question: Who is barefoot, dumb, and lethargic?

troglodyte

TROG-luh-dyte

n. a backwards or secluded person who is oblivious to the world

Perhaps the American election system should be revamped to compensate for the **troglodytes** who cast votes for whichever candidate the mainstream media throws its weight behind.

truculent

TRUCK-you-lent

adj. eager to fight; defiant

The mustachioed immigration advocate entered the No Spin Zone in a **truculent** mood and promptly got the fight he was seeking.

unctuous

UNK-choo-us

adj. insincere; slick

The professional athlete's **unctuous** refusal of a multi-million dollar contract didn't sit well with fans of the game who already think the players are overpaid.

vacillate

VASS-uh-late

v. to waver back and forth on a decision

Depending on the audience, an obsequious politician can **vacillate** between advocating fiscal discipline and promising new spending.

vacuous

VACK-you-us

adj. vapid; air-headed

It was shocking to see the usually **vacuous** starlet featured in a thoughtful, poignant PSA about the need for respectful dissent in debates about social issues among Americans.

vainglorious

veyn-GLOR-ee-us

adj. egotistical; conceited

The most dangerous place to stand is between a **vainglorious** man and a mirror.

varlet

VAR-let

n. a rogue; a deceitful scoundrel

Most Americans are fed up with back-room politics being conducted by **varlets** whose primary concern is whether they'll get sent back to Washington after the next election.

venomous

VEN-uh-muhs

adj. hostile; hateful

Loony left-wingers seem to unleash their most **venomous** attacks on female conservatives.

verbose

vur-BOSE

adj. overly wordy

Don't give your humble correspondent a headache by sending **verbose** letters to read on the air—you've got to keep it pithy!

verecund

VER-i-kund

adj. modest; shy

It's not uncommon for a **verecund** child to blossom into a confident and extroverted adult.

vexation

veck-SAY-shun

n. a state of agitation or annoyance

There was excessive **vexation** in Chicago after a Cubs fan interfered with a ball in play, leading to the team's painful loss in the playoffs.

vilipend

VIL-uh-pend

v. to disparage or deride

Some observers believe our political decline began in 1987 when Ted Kennedy took to the Senate floor to **vilipend** Judge Robert Bork.

virago

vi-RAH-goh

n. a nag; a harpy

Critics of Michelle Obama's anti-obesity campaign accuse the First Lady of acting like a **virago**, telling Americans what they can and cannot eat.

visigoth

VIZ-i-goth

n. a barbarian

The swells in Garden City loathed
kids from Levittown, viewing them as nothing more
than a bunch of crude **visigoths**.

vituperative

vie-TOO-pur-uh-tiv

adj. scathing; abusive

Friends of O.J. and Nicole Brown Simpson often worried about her safety because of the overtly **vituperative** nature of their very public fights.

vociferous

vo–SIFF–ur–us

adj. noisy; boisterous

Nothing can spoil a movie quite like a bunch of **vociferous** teens.

wisenheimer

WY-zen-hy-mur

n. a smart alec; a bigmouth

During his bitter dispute with NBC about whether he would continue hosting "The Tonight Show," **wisenheimer** Conan O'Brien took to the airwaves with some nasty jokes about his employer.